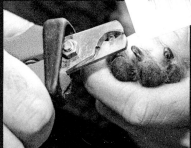

DOG GROOMER

BEAUTIFYING MAN'S BEST FRIEND

Christie Marlowe and Andrew Morkes

MASON CREST
PHILADELPHIA
MIAMI

Mason Crest
450 Parkway Drive, Suite D
Broomall, Pennsylvania 19008
(866) MCP-BOOK (toll-free)
www.masoncrest.com

First printing
9 8 7 6 5 4 3 2 1

ISBN (hardback) 978-1-4222-4325-1
ISBN (series) 978-1-4222-4319-0
ISBN (ebook) 978-1-4222-7489-7

Cataloging in Publication Data on file with the publisher.

NATIONAL
HIGHLIGHTS

Developed and Produced by National Highlights, Inc.
Editor: Andrew Gance
Interior and cover design: Jana Rade, impact studios
Interior layout: Tara Raymo, CreativelyTara
Production: Michelle Luke
Proofreader: Abby Jaworski

QR CODES AND LINKS TO THIRD-PARTY CONTENT

KEY ICONS TO LOOK FOR:

WORDS TO UNDERSTAND: These words with their easy-to-understand definitions will increase the reader's understanding of the text while building vocabulary skills.

SIDEBARS: This boxed material within the main text allows readers to build knowledge, gain insights, explore possibilities, and broaden their perspectives by weaving together additional information to provide realistic and holistic perspectives.

EDUCATIONAL VIDEOS: Readers can view videos by scanning our QR codes, providing them with additional educational content to supplement the text. Examples include news coverage, moments in history, speeches, iconic sports moments, and much more!

TEXT-DEPENDENT QUESTIONS: These questions send the reader back to the text for more careful attention to the evidence presented there.

RESEARCH PROJECTS: Readers are pointed toward areas of further inquiry connected to each chapter. Suggestions are provided for projects that encourage deeper research and analysis.

SERIES GLOSSARY OF KEY TERMS: This back-of-the-book glossary contains terminology used throughout this series. Words found here increase the reader's ability to read and comprehend higher-level books and articles in this field.

WORDS TO UNDERSTAND

breeding: controlling how animals mate to create a desired outcome

euthanized: killed a living organism peacefully and painlessly

hygienic: something that is clean and will not cause disease

unconditional: without limits or requirements

CHAPTER 1

HUMANS AND THEIR DOGS

MAN'S BEST FRIEND

The nickname "man's best friend" is more than appropriate considering the long history humans and dogs share. Dogs were the first animals to be domesticated. In other words, they underwent the process where a population of animals or plants is changed through years of **breeding** in order to emphasize traits that benefit humans. Other examples of domesticated animals include sheep, cattle, pigs, and chickens. Dogs, a domesticated species of the gray wolf, are the most widely kept working, hunting, and pet animal in human history. The dogs we know and love today are a part of our lives because the gray wolf was domesticated nearly 33,000 years ago!

Why and how domestication came about is widely debated, but most people agree that the relationship between dogs and humans, especially in the early

Dogs are some of the most popular pets because they bring immense joy to their owners.

stages of domestication, was beneficial (helpful) to both species. Dogs would have been provided with safety by living in human camps, a more reliable food source, and more chances to breed. Humans, on the other hand, would have benefited from improved sanitation (from dogs cleaning up their food scraps), warmth (from the dogs' bodies and fur), and safety (a barking dog could alert them to danger, for example). More importantly, the presence of a dog would have greatly improved the chances for success when hunting. Dr. Jonica Newby, a former veterinarian and science writer, even suggests that the domestication of dogs is one of the main reasons that humans as a species have succeeded as well as they have!

Since canines were domesticated, the relationship between dogs and humans has come a long way. Over the years, they have been bred for herding other domesticated animals, hunting, controlling rodent (rats, mice, etc.)

populations, guarding, helping fishermen with nets, detecting (such as sniffing for bombs or drugs), and pulling loads (sled dogs, for example). In recent times, dogs have added to their job duties by assisting individuals with physical or mental disabilities. For example, there are now guide dogs for people who have impaired vision or who are completely blind.

However, the large majority of all dogs are kept as pets. Before World War II, keeping dogs as pets was most often a practice of upper-class men and women, but since World War II (1939–1945), the pet population has grown significantly. Americans own nearly 90 million dogs and 60 percent of all households own at least one or more dogs, according to the American Pet Products Association.

And that leads to job opportunities! After all, dogs need care. They need medical attention from veterinarians. They may need training from professional animal trainers. And they need grooming.

Learn more about what it's like to own a dog grooming business.

DOG GROOMERS

"For many people, their pet is just another member of the family," says Rheya Zimmerman, an experienced dog groomer with more than twenty years in the industry. "This is especially true for their dogs."

Rheya is right. According to researcher Emma Powers, "The last fifty years have seen dogs increasingly drawn into the home as family members." She even writes that owners describe their dogs as "furry children" to emphasize "the time spent caring for dogs." Considering the shared history of dogs and humans and the many ways that we have helped each other grow and survive as a species, it's really not all that surprising they've finally been assigned significant roles as members of the family!

Working as a dog groomer is a great career for people who like to be their own boss and have flexible work hours.

"When dogs are considered a luxury, or 'just something nice to have,'" Rheya says, "people are less willing to spend money for their well-being. Today, they are family members—and people will do what it takes to take care of family members."

Pet care workers, such as this dog groomer, often report high levels of job satisfaction.

This is where groomers come in. Dog grooming is the process of **hygienic** care and cleaning of a dog. It "is an important part of dog care," Rheya says. Regular grooming helps to make sure that a dog is healthy and comfortable. "Depending on the breed, age, and health of the dog," she continues, "grooming can be required daily." Many breeds, however, require significantly less grooming than this.

A dog breed is a group of closely related and visibly similar dogs. The many breeds of dogs that we know today—Labrador retrievers, German shepherds, and golden retrievers being the three most popular examples in the United States—were developed through years of breeding. Labrador retrievers, for example, get their name from the purpose for which they were originally bred. Retrievers are a kind of hunting dog, typically used when hunting for birds such as ducks and geese. Retrievers were bred to fetch the birds once a hunter shot them.

German shepherds are the second most popular dog breed in the United States.

"Certain breeds require grooming almost constantly," Rheya says. Many dog breeds lose and regrow hair year-round in a process called shedding. Other breeds, such as poodles, "molt," or lose their hair only once or twice a year. These kinds of breeds require grooming by a professional every six to eight weeks.

"How often you *have* to groom a dog," Rheya says, "depends on a lot. But no matter the circumstances, having your dog groomed will always be good for a dog's physical and emotional health." According to Rheya, one reason owners have their dog groomed is to build a closer bond. "Bringing your pet to a groomer is one way to show that you care about your dog," she says.

It takes training and many skills to become a dog groomer, but one thing that this career does *not* require is a college education!

THE COLLEGE QUESTION

"When I was thinking about going to college," Rheya says, "a college education wasn't considered as important as it is today. College then was a way to get skills, not the only way to get skills."

As Rheya suggests, many people today do see college as the only way to find a stable, well-paying career. This is part of the reason that in 2016, nearly seven out of every ten students in the United States who graduated from high school went on to attend college, according to the U.S. Department of Labor.

Unfortunately, a college education isn't necessarily a safe bet when it comes to finding a successful career. The *Wall Street Journal* reports that students who graduated from college with debt (money owed to a person, company, or organization) had average debt of $37,712. This much debt takes more than ten years to pay off! Additionally, studies have shown that some college graduates cannot find a job that is a good match for their degree or they can only find jobs that don't require a college degree!

THE MOST POPULAR DOG BREEDS IN THE UNITED STATES, 2017

1. Labrador retrievers
2. German shepherds
3. Golden retrievers
4. French bulldogs
5. Bulldogs
6. Beagles
7. Poodles
8. Rottweilers
9. Yorkshire terriers
10. German shorthaired pointers

Source: American Kennel Club

USING VOLUNTEERING TO ANSWER
THE COLLEGE QUESTION

"I always loved animals," Rheya says, explaining how she originally became interested in grooming dogs. "Animals are wonderful," she continues, "especially dogs. They provide **unconditional** love. They don't care what you look like, how much money you make, what color your skin is, or what gender you are. All that dogs care about is whether or not you are kind to them."

While she was in high school, Rheya volunteered at local animal shelters. "This was much more than just getting experience," she says. "At the facility where I worked, we took dogs, puppies, cats, and kittens from shelters where they were about to be **euthanized**. We worked with them, played with them, taught them basic commands, cared for their needs, and if they were sick, we did our best to get them well so they could be sent to adoption centers to find loving homes. [An adoption center is a facility where dogs, cats, and other animals are matched with qualified and loving owners.]

FAST FACT

While the domestication of dogs has been going on for many thousands of years, most dog breeds are at most a few hundred years old.

We worked very hard to make the animals adoptable so they could give many years of love and loyalty to new owners."

This volunteer experience Rheya had during high school would shape the course of her professional life. It helped her see what she wanted to do with her life—and it showed her that a college education was not necessary for her to achieve her dreams.

High school is an influential time for most young people. Both in and out of their classes, young people have opportunities to explore their interests. By this time, many students are old enough to begin to explore old hobbies more deeply or take on new ones. Rheya's time

You do not have to attend a four-year college to be successful in life.

at the animal shelter, for example, allowed her to build on an interest she'd had since she was a young child. It gave her valuable knowledge for her future career and allowed her to grow her passion for working with and comforting animals.

"When you work with animals," she says, "you have to be extremely calm. They can sense if you are afraid and will bite or jump in order to defend themselves. Working with difficult dogs in the shelter was a great way to begin to learn how to be confident around aggressive or fearful dogs."

Even today, Rheya spends much of her free time volunteering at animal shelters and advocating for pet adoption agencies. (When you volunteer, you help out at an organization for free. You do so because you want to help people and make the world a better place.) "Only about 30 percent of cats and dogs are adopted from shelters or animal rescues," Rheya says. "Millions of dogs and cats a year are euthanized. Dogs and cats that are owned live longer, healthier lives than strays or those in shelters. Animals love us and need love. That's why I still volunteer at shelters—and it's the same reason why I became a dog groomer."

For Rheya, a college education was not nearly as important as doing something that she loves. But doing what you love doesn't mean you necessarily need to settle for a smaller paycheck! According to the American Pet Products Association, Americans spent $66.8 billion on their pets in 2016. Spending in this area has increased each year since 2008. This means that there are growing opportunities for dog groomers like Rheya.

So should you go to college? It is an important question. There are a lot of options out there, and one of the best decisions that anyone can make is to get educated about education. Ask yourself these questions: What do I love to do? What are my hobbies? What do I have a passion for? Do I need to go to college to get the skills that I need to be successful? If I decide to become a dog groomer, would it make sense to earn a degree in business (or at least take a few business classes) so that I'm better qualified to run my business? How can I earn a living doing what I love? Will working as a dog groomer generate enough money for me to have a comfortable life, or do I need to obtain extra education and skills in another field?

Take some time to think about these and other questions. Consider volunteering in the animal care field like Rheya did. Ask your parents, school counselors, and teachers for advice. Talking to a dog groomer about the pros and cons of their field will also help you make an educated decision. The more information that you have, the easier it will be to choose a career path.

Volunteering at a dog grooming business is a great way to learn more about this career. Above, a high school student tries her hand at grooming a poodle.

RESEARCH PROJECT

Create a list of careers that you're interested in (e.g., dog groomer, pet store owner, etc.). Learn what the educational requirements and job duties are for each career. Then create a list of pluses and minuses for each occupation. This will help you to decide which is the best fit for your interests and educational goals.

TEXT-DEPENDENT QUESTIONS

1. What is domestication, and what are some examples of domesticated animals?
2. What is the average student loan debt for college graduates?
3. How did Rheya's volunteer work help her to determine her career path?

WORDS TO UNDERSTAND

infestation: an invasion of insects, parasites, or other unwanted living things

monitoring: watching and keeping track of something

optional: something that doesn't have to be done; it is not required

susceptible: likely to be influenced or harmed by a particular thing, such as an emotion or disease

CHAPTER 2

WHAT DO DOG GROOMERS DO?

THE IMPORTANCE OF DOG GROOMING

According to Jan DeAngelo, there are many reasons to have your dog groomed. Jan has been grooming dogs for about eight years and works at a shop that specializes in creative grooming—a style that's different from traditional methods because it commonly involves artificial colors and nontraditional cuts. Making dogs look like other animals such as horses, giraffes, or pandas involves some common creative cuts. Traditional dog grooming, on the other hand, gives dogs one of a number of cuts considered appropriate for a specific breed.

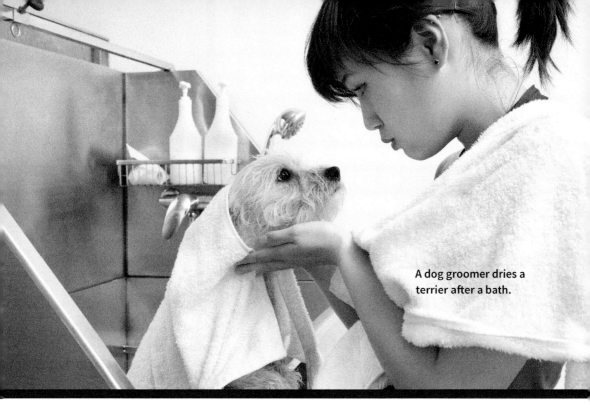

A dog groomer dries a terrier after a bath.

"I started working at this shop because I liked the freedom that creative grooming gives a groomer," Jan says. "But creative grooming is really only a small part of our business, since it defeats many of the practical reasons that someone would want or need to get their dogs groomed. Most clients come to us for traditional grooming and will occasionally get some pet tuning on holidays or special occasions." Pet tuning is a simpler form of creative grooming offered at usually a fraction of the cost of a creative cut. Pet tuning can be a great way for owners to have a hand in stylizing their dog, and it can build a stronger bond between a dog and owner.

The reasons to have a dog groomed include the following:

- decreasing the chances of various health problems such as thrush (a fungal infection), scratches, and other skin problems
- cleaning the pet's skin and coat

- monitoring the dog's health by checking for cuts, heat (a stage in a female dog's reproductive cycle in which she becomes receptive to mating), swelling (which can indicate disease or infection), or changes in mood (which could indicate illness)
- building a closer bond between an owner and their dog
- reducing the chances of infestation by parasites such as fleas, ticks, or tapeworms

"Dogs are a part of the family," Jan says, "and grooming is good for both the owners and the pet." Grooming makes a dog more comfortable, happy, and healthy. A clean dog is one that can be cuddled. Since dogs cannot talk, they and their owners communicate through other senses, such as touch." Not only does grooming make a dog a cleaner presence in its owner's home, but it also protects the health of the human members of the family. Many of the kinds of parasites and diseases to which dogs are susceptible can be passed from dogs to humans.

FUN DOG FACTS

- Dogs dream just like humans. Older dogs and puppies dream more frequently than middle-aged adult dogs.
- A dog's nose has as many as 300 million receptors. Human noses only have about five million receptors.
- Rin Tin Tin, the famous German shepherd that appeared in television shows and movies, was nominated for an Academy Award.
- Petting a dog is good for both humans and the dog. Both of their blood pressures decrease when petting occurs.
- Seventy percent of dog owners sign their dog's name on their holiday cards.

Source: American Kennel Club

GROOMING A DOG

Dog grooming might sound like a simple job, but a lot of hard work is required to do even a traditional groom.

CUSTOMER SERVICE

"A groomer is responsible for customer service [talking with and otherwise assisting customers], client relationships, and animal care, among other things," Jan says. "The most important job that a groomer is responsible for, though, is making sure that the dog remains safe while it is in your care. Customers can be a nightmare in any business, but I can't imagine anything worse than a customer whose dog was injured while in the care of a groomer."

FLEA FACTS

- A female flea can lay up to fifty eggs per day, but most lay about twenty on average.
- Fleas are considered some of the best jumpers in the world. They can leap more than 150 times their body length.
- Fleas transmit diseases that affect humans. They can transmit bacteria that causes cat scratch disease, which can result in fatigue, headaches, a low-grade fever, and body aches.
- Fleas can transmit parasites such as tapeworms to dogs and other animals. The tapeworm lives in the animal's intestine and can cause nausea, weakness, diarrhea, hunger or loss of appetite, fatigue, weight loss, and abdominal pain.

Sources: PetMD.com, WebMD.com

Fleas can transmit diseases to dogs that can cause weakness, diarrhea, loss of appetite, and other negative side effects.

Before any groomer begins to groom a dog, they must deal with the customers. After a groomer meets the dog and owner, they have to find out how the owner wants the dog to look once groomed and when the owner wants to pick up their pet. Inspecting the dog is also an important part of the intake process. Intake occurs when a client is greeted and their information is taken down at the beginning of the appointment. It's important to create a written record of what the customer wants for their dog, the condition of the dog before grooming begins, and agreed-upon prices and services so that there is no misunderstanding between the groomer and the customer.

"Dogs, especially those that aren't groomed often," Jan says, "can come in with all sorts of issues that can affect the final grooming price. If they have fleas or mites, they will need to be washed with a special flea shampoo. This can be expensive stuff and usually requires an additional fee. Having some on hand to sell to a customer is a good idea, but flea shampoo isn't meant to be a permanent solution for dogs. Fleas often live in the home. Educating customers about fleas gives them a chance to begin to take care of the issue before they bring the dog home."

According to Jan, another issue that should be addressed with a customer is "matting." Matted fur is too tangled to be combed out and restored, so it must be cut off and allowed to regrow. "Some customers really hate to hear that their dogs have matted fur. They'll try to refuse to have the matted fur cut off. Matted fur can be uncomfortable for a dog, though. Besides, matted fur is almost always dirty fur. Owners are better off having that fur removed from their pets. Groomers save themselves big headaches by going over issues like these before letting a customer leave. Customers don't like surprises!"

THE GROOMING PROCESS

Once a groomer has determined what kind of cut they are giving a dog and if any other issues need to be addressed, they begin by pre-cutting the dog. This involves removing the excess or matted hair. Pre-cutting is important because it allows the shampoo to better penetrate the fur to reach the dog's skin.

After pre-cutting, a dog is bathed and dried. While bathing a dog, groomers will take care of removing any excess or shedding hair that wasn't removed during the pre-cut. They also clean the dog's ears and express the dog's anal glands. This is a technique that involves squeezing the glands located on either side of a dog's anus to release the contents. It is an important part of making sure that a dog is clean and comfortable.

"Some groomers prefer to cage dry a dog," Jan says, "in order to bathe or groom other dogs while the dog is drying. But I prefer to hand dry the dogs. Cage drying, depending on the breed and age of the dog, can be uncomfortable and even dangerous. Some dogs have died because the groomer got distracted

Dog groomers discuss their work.

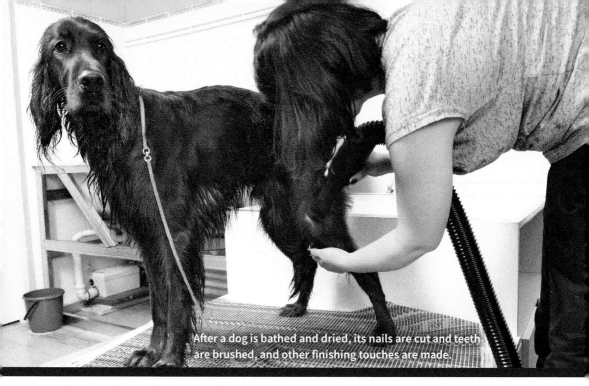

After a dog is bathed and dried, its nails are cut and teeth are brushed, and other finishing touches are made.

with something else and left the dog in the cage dryer too long." A cage dryer is a special kind of cage that uses a combination of heat and fans to dry a dog. There are many models available, and some are considered more dangerous than others.

Once a dog is bathed and dried, its nails are cut, teeth are brushed, and ears are cleaned, and any other finishing touches are made. If the owner requests them, perfume, bows, or a bandana can be added. "At this point, the grooming is complete," Jan says, "but the dogs must still be cared for. They will need to be given water, taken out for a short walk to use the bathroom, and then put into a kennel or some other safe area to wait for their owners to pick them up."

DOG TATTOOS

One dog grooming fad is dog tattoos. Traditional tattoos (for humans) are permanent and are inked directly into the skin, but dog tattoos are airbrushed onto a dog's fur using a stencil and a special pet-friendly dye. These tattoos come in a variety of formats and are used by owners who want to advertise a business, sports fans who want to show off their team allegiance, or pet owners who simply want to extend the gift of style to their four-legged companions.

OTHER SERVICES AND RESPONSIBILITIES

While the bathing and grooming process makes up most of the work that a dog groomer is paid to do, there are other tasks and services dog groomers do that are either optional for a customer or required for the business. Grooming can

Some groomers try to expand their client base by offering dog walking services.

be a very messy business, for example, and after a day of grooming is done, a groomer will need to sweep hair, wrap up electric cords, and sterilize (make free of germs) tools so that they are ready for the next day.

"Don't forget," Jan says, "that in order to make enough money, a groomer will need to groom multiple dogs a day. If you're working alone, without any employees, this means you will need to answer phones and emails, check in and check out dogs, and care for all of the other animals in the shop." Groomers need to be able to multitask (do many different things at once) in order to make it all work.

There are many other services that are commonly offered by dog groomers that can be great ways for groomers to make some extra money without doing much additional work. One of these services involves "kenneling," or allowing dogs to stay in your cages for an extended period of time while their owners are away.

"Most shops also sell some pet care products," Jan says, "in order to make some extra money. What kinds of goods you carry generally depends on who your clients are. Most shops carry dog treats, for example. Other shops, like mine, are located in big cities, which means we often have more clients than we can handle. So we sell some simpler versions of the tools we use. That way, owners can do some grooming at home for themselves. This may not be the best idea for every shop, though. If you have fewer clients, you won't want your customers grooming their dogs themselves."

Some dog groomers also choose to offer dog walking and vacation pet care services (called boarding) when they are not performing their grooming duties. This allows them to make more money while still being around dogs.

Dog groomers' most important responsibility, of course, is making sure that a dog remains comfortable and safe while in their care. "This is much harder than it sounds," Jan says. He says that some dogs become very stressed when they are in the care of a groomer. "Bites can happen," he admits, "but a good groomer knows when a dog is feeling fear or anxiety. We can tell when dogs are about to become aggressive or react. That's really a vital skill to have. It wouldn't be such a problem if the groomer were the only one who could get hurt. I don't want to get bit, but I can cope with it. What's worse, though, is if a dog hurts itself. Like if a dog jumps when I have a pair of scissors in my hand, the dog can end up badly hurt. That's not something I want happening, ever. I'd much rather deal with my own blood than explain to an owner why her dog is bleeding!"

Some dog groomers also provide cat grooming services.

A groomer provides health, safety, and happiness to a dog and owner. The most successful groomers are the ones who truly care for each dog, even if that means a few nips from scared animals and a few difficult customers now and then!

ADDITIONAL OPPORTUNITIES FOR DOG GROOMERS

Some dog groomers offer grooming services for other animals, such as cats. Some groomers even provide grooming services for guinea pigs and other rodents. Groomers may also be hired to clip the nails of lizards and other reptiles. If you're up for the challenge, it makes sense to learn how to groom as many types of animals as possible. Doing so will add up to more money and more customers. And that's nothing to bark at!

ADVANCEMENT OPPORTUNITIES

If you work at a job for a while, you'll get the chance for advancement. Workers advance in their jobs by receiving a promotion (a move to a higher-level position), managerial duties overseeing other workers, and a higher salary. In the dog grooming field, advancement is available but limited. Making more money will always be available to groomers who are willing to open their own dog grooming businesses. And you may be asked to supervise other groomers. Becoming a business owner, however, can be a lot of responsibility and stress that may not be worth the extra money for some people.

Opening a successful business is also dependent on where a groomer lives. One grooming business may be more than enough for a small rural town. A city, on the other hand, will offer plenty of chances to open grooming businesses—but at the same time, the cost of living (how much it costs for food, rent, etc.) and working in many cities can be staggering. Similarly, a city will likely have more grooming businesses with which a new business must compete.

Many skills and years of experience will likely be needed before someone is ready to open their own shop. To be a successful business owner, you need to master the basics of finance (the way money is managed by an individual or a business) and organization. You need to be able to do basic bookkeeping on income and expenditures (money spent to run a business or for another reason). Bookkeeping is how people keep track of a business's money; it is also called accounting.

You'll need to know about the tax and business laws that apply to your business, and you'll need to organize insurance, pay bills, and track invoices (bills that you send to customers if they don't pay at the time of service). Taxes are the money that you are required to pay to the government in order to operate a business and for other reasons. Insurance is a type of business arrangement

TALL AND SHORT

Zeus was the tallest dog ever measured. This Great Dane from Otsego, Michigan, measured an incredible 44 inches (111.8 centimeters) from foot to withers. He was the same size as an average-size donkey. Zeus weighed 155 pounds (70.3 kilograms) and ate twelve cups of food a day. He died in 2014 but left his owners with many happy—and big—memories.

The smallest dog in terms of height is a female Chihuahua named Milly. She measured 3.8 inches tall (9.65 centimeters) on February 21, 2013—about the height of a high-heel shoe. Milly lives in Cuba.

Source: Guinness World Records

Owning a dog grooming business is a great choice for those with strong business, marketing, and customer-service skills.

in which a person or business pays a certain amount of money to an insurance agency in exchange for being paid back at a later time if loss, damage, illness, or other bad things happen to them or their business.

Groomers can learn many business skills in order to earn more money and become more successful. Some groomers, such as Jan, learn how to groom creatively. He is a member of the National Association of Professional Creative Groomers, which holds annual contests for creative groomers where they can show off their grooming masterpieces and earn fame for their grooming abilities. Being able to prove your skill to your customers will give them a reason to come back and a reason to pay more money for your services. So while "advancement" might not be available to dog groomers in the same way it is in other career paths, that is no reason for groomers to ever stop learning and developing their skills. The more skills you have—whatever your career—the more valuable your services will be!

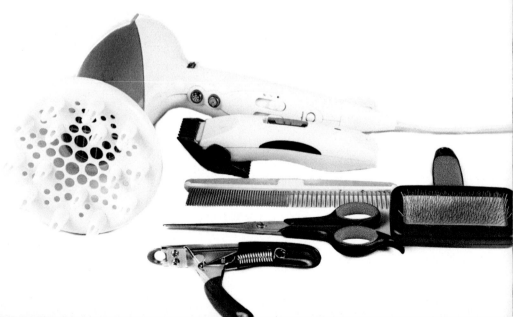

RESEARCH PROJECT

Take your dog to a grooming shop and observe the various steps in the dog grooming process. (If you don't have a dog, ask your friend if you can borrow their dog.) What did you like and dislike about the process? Is this something that you think you could do as a career? If so, write a 250-word essay that details why this occupation is a good match for your interests and skills.

TEXT-DEPENDENT QUESTIONS

1. Why should people groom their dogs?
2. What is pre-cutting?
3. How can dog groomers earn extra money?

CHAPTER 3

TERMS OF THE TRADE

breed: The looks and characteristics of a dog that make it part of a unique group, such as American foxhounds, German shepherds, or Havanese. It's estimated that there are more than 340 dog breeds known throughout the world, but the American Kennel Club recognizes only 192 breeds.

breed standard: An agreed-upon set of guidelines to help define the looks and characteristics of each individual breed.

bristle brush: A brush that is used for dogs with short or wiry coats.

brush: A grooming tool that is used on a dog's coat.

cage dryer: A dryer that attaches to the kennel to dry the dog; this drying method is used for dogs that cannot be dried in other ways.

carding: The process of using a blunt-edged tool to remove the loose, dead undercoat on a dog.

clean face: A grooming technique in which the face, cheeks, and muzzle of a dog are shaved very close to the skin.

clean feet: A grooming technique in which the feet are completely shaved, exposing the nails and the entire foot up to the ankle.

clippers: A razor-styled hand tool that is used to reduce the length of a dog's coat.

coat: The hair that covers a dog's body. The coat may be a double coat, which has a soft undercoat and a tougher topcoat, or a single coat, which does not have an undercoat.

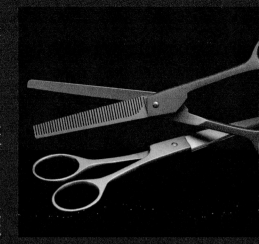

comb: A grooming tool that is used to make a dog's coat look attractive. Medium-toothed combs are a good general-use comb, but groomers should use a fine-toothed comb for a dog with thin hair and a wide-toothed comb if the dog's hair is thick.

creative grooming: A style of dog grooming that's different from traditional grooming because it commonly involves artificial colors and nontraditional cuts.

de-matting: Removing matted fur.

dry bathing: Bathing and cleaning techniques that do not use water. Examples include dry shampoo, pet wipes, and freshening sprays or foams.

ear cleanser: A veterinarian-recommended commercial cleaning solution that is used to clean a dog's ears.

flea comb: A special comb that is used to remove fleas and tangles.

forced-air dryer: A drying machine that is used to completely dry the dog's fur after towel-drying.

furnishings: A grooming technique in which the excess hair on the dog's legs, tail, head, and face are groomed in a manner that complements its coat.

hand stripping and plucking: The process of using one's fingers or stripping tools to remove the dead outer coat of wire haired breeds (such as terriers).

hot spots: Red, sore patches of skin on a dog, often accompanied by some hair loss. Hot spots are caused by parasites, allergies, or poor grooming habits.

kennel: A small shelter for a dog, cat, or other animal. It is used to safely house the dog before and after it is groomed, during transit, and for other reasons when the pet cannot be in its home.

matted hair: A mass of extremely tangled and interwoven hair. Matting can be caused by the dog's hair type, friction, and poor grooming habits.

molting: When an animal loses its hair, feathers, skin, or shell to make way for new growth.

nail grinder: An electric-powered tool that uses a small, rotating head to wear down a dog's nails through the use of friction.

parasite: An organism that lives on or inside another organism to obtain nutrients from it. Fleas and ticks are examples of parasites that live on dogs and cats. They live off of the blood of the host animal.

pin brush: Similar to a slicker brush, but this brush's wire pins are tipped with rubber or plastic and are used to brush dogs that have longer, silkier coats.

pre-cutting: The process of removing the excess or matted hair on a dog before the main cut is given. Pre-cutting is important because it allows the shampoo to better penetrate the fur to reach a dog's skin.

the quick: A slang term for a blood vessel that protrudes into the main area of a dog's nail. Groomers must be very careful that they do not pierce this blood vessel when nail clipping or grinding.

rolling the coat: A grooming technique that involves regular, repeated hand stripping and/or carding to keep the dog's coat well groomed and in shape.

scissoring: A grooming technique that uses a metal comb and scissors to complete and finish a trim. This technique is used for finishing trim work on a dog's feet, face, and tail areas, or when the dog's owner requests that the dog be trimmed longer than a clipper blade will allow.

shaving in reverse: Shaving against the grain of the dog's hair, or from the back of the dog toward the front.

shedding: When a dog loses its hair—most often during the spring and fall, but also when it is stressed, affected by environmental issues, or has a skin irritation.

shedding blade: This is not an actual cutting tool, but a horseshoe-shaped comb with small, harmless teeth. It is used on short, flat, or combination coats to remove loose fur.

slicker brush: A type of brush with a flat or curved head. It has rows of thin wire pins that can be used with all coat types and is used to remove loose fur and help detangle.

styptic powder: Medication that is used to stop bleeding, such as which occurs during nail clipping.

undercoat: The soft coat that is located under a tougher top coat on a dog that has a double coat.

undercoat rake: This grooming tool is similar to a pin brush, but it has fewer and longer pins. It is used to groom dogs with double and heavy coats.

WORDS TO UNDERSTAND

certification: a credential that is awarded by an association or other industry organization to a worker who completes educational training, passes a test, and meets other requirements that show that they are highly skilled

negotiate: when two groups or individuals seek to reach an agreement on a topic they disagree on

strategize: the process of making a plan to achieve a goal

veteran: someone who has had a lot of experience in a certain job; it may also mean someone who has served in the military

CHAPTER 4

PREPARING FOR THE FIELD AND MAKING A LIVING

BECOMING A DOG GROOMER

"Becoming a groomer is a pretty simple process," says Manuel, a relatively new groomer with only a few years working in the field. "The most difficult part is finding training." While the law does not regulate dog groomers and no **certification** is needed to become a groomer, it is still absolutely necessary to get training. "If you just open up a shop without knowing what you're doing," Manuel comments, "your customers will figure it out pretty quick. Your business won't last long."

Some young people prepare to become dog groomers by participating in an apprenticeship.

APPRENTICESHIPS

One of the most popular ways to learn how to groom dogs is to become an apprentice to a **veteran** groomer. According to Manuel, some groomers will allow you to pay them for training as an apprentice. The price and length of the training typically depends on how much experience the groomer has. According to the U.S. Department of Labor, most grooming apprenticeships last between twelve and twenty weeks.

While paying for apprenticeship is one way to get training, Manuel says that he didn't have to pay for his training at all. "The shop that I began working at needed an extra pair of hands. So I asked if I could be trained while I worked a job for free." Manuel began his career washing dogs in the shop where he was working, and he received training instead of a paycheck. "Some people I know,"

Manuel says, "even found paid apprenticeships. They got a small paycheck for the work they did—and they got all of the training they needed at the same time."

Some large pet supply and pet care companies such as PetSmart and Petco also provide paid and unpaid apprenticeship opportunities. The best ways to learn more about these programs are to visit these organizations' websites and stop in at a store near you to talk to a manager about training opportunities.

GROOMING SCHOOLS, ONLINE CLASSES, AND CERTIFICATION

Other options include going to a grooming school or taking online dog grooming classes. Most programs such as these end in a certification from the National Dog Groomers Association of America (NDGAA). According to Manuel, these school and online classes can be good, but they sometimes offer little hands-on training, so they should be combined with other experience. To become certified

Discover what goes on in dog grooming courses at The College of Animal Welfare in the United Kingdom.

by the NDGAA, you will need to attend at least one workshop and take two tests—one that is written and one that demonstrates a groomer's practical skills. Demonstrating your practical skills requires grooming four different breeds, one from each of the four major kinds of breeds: sporting, non-sporting, short-legged terriers, and long-legged terriers. Certification can be a way to prove to employers that you have the skills you need to begin a career as a groomer and be able to **negotiate** a better wage. But, according to Manuel, some schools like this can be expensive—and certification is not required to be successful as a groomer.

A student at a dog grooming school practices her technique.

TRAINING WITH PET CARE COMPANIES

Many pet supply and pet care companies such as Petco offer a combination of hands-on experience and classroom education when training new groomers. This type of training may be classified as an apprenticeship (as discussed earlier in this chapter) or simply consist of informal on-the-job training. Manuel warns, however, that the other two options should be explored first before seeking training from a corporate store. "Large pet stores kind of have a bad reputation. That means getting employed anywhere else can be difficult if this is where you were trained."

No matter how you get the skills you need, though, compared to a college education, the small investment of time and money means you could soon be qualified for an exciting career as a dog groomer!

HOW MUCH CAN I MAKE?

Because the majority of dog groomers are self-employed, it can be very difficult to say how much money the average dog groomer earns in a year. (To be self-employed means that you are not paid regular wages by an employer, but instead, you work for yourself.)

"Multiple dog groomers might work at a single dog grooming business," says Hannah Singleton, "but most or all of them will be considered self-employed because most dog groomers work for commissions." This means they are paid a certain percentage of every groom that they complete. Hannah is the owner of a dog grooming business; she says she has been working as a groomer for "at least fifteen years now."

According to Hannah, there are positives and negatives about being self-employed. On the one hand, being self-employed allows a groomer to set their own working hours, and it gives a groomer some control over how much they charge for grooming. On the other hand, being self-employed means that a regular income is not guaranteed, and that certain benefits, such as health insurance, which would usually be paid for in full or in part by an employer, need to be paid for by the self-employed person.

"At my shop," Hannah says, "I offer an hourly wage to all the groomers who work with me. On top of that, I give all groomers 50 percent of whatever they make grooming. This means that groomers who work for me are not technically self-employed but they get the benefits of being self-employed. At the same time, they know they will definitely get a paycheck even during a slow week. I think my shop is rare, though. Anyone thinking of getting into the business should understand that they'll be working mostly off commissions. Unless they open their own business, of course."

HIGH-LEVEL EARNINGS

Dog groomers who own their own grooming business, like Hannah, have the potential to make a good living. Hannah not only owns the business, but she also works as a groomer. This means that for every groom she completes, she is able to keep 100 percent of the profits.

"Because of the way I pay the other groomers in the shop," Hannah says, "I make slightly less money than I would otherwise. But we are a good business, so we are usually booked solid almost the whole year-round. I'm pretty sure that whatever I lose from my own income is gained back because of the fact that my groomers are happy." According to Hannah, happy groomers mean happy animals—and happy animals mean happy owners. Happy owners come back more often and are more likely to tip. A tip is a gift of money that a customer gives a service professional if they provide above-average service.

"Tips," Hannah says, "are a pretty big part of dog grooming. They are usually not factored in when people talk about how much they make a year." A fast groomer can finish up to about nine grooms a day, and according to Hannah, about 80 percent of her customers tip. "My regulars tip almost every time," she says. By "regulars," Hannah means repeat customers who are happy with the service she provides.

So what does all that mean? If Hannah charges on average $45 for each grooming, she could make $405 a day (for nine grooming jobs) just from the dogs she grooms herself. (Note: Groomers charge an average of $25 to $90 per dog, based on the animal's size and other factors.) Then you add onto that the tips she makes, which could be another $55 or more a day. Now she's earning

A dog groomer prepares a canine for a dog show in Italy. Groomers can earn extra income by working at such shows.

Dog groomers who operate their own businesses have the opportunity to earn a higher income than those who work at salons or pet stores.

$460 a day—or as much as $2,300 for a five-day week! And that doesn't include the money she gets from her employees' jobs. But before you start counting your money, keep in mind that not every groomer works that fast. You may only be able to groom six dogs a day, which will reduce your income.

The U.S. Department of Labor lists customer service skills as important for any dog groomer to have, and as Hannah suggests, good customer service skills will lead to more money and more tips. It makes sense, because if you're nice to people, take the time to explain your services and fees to customers, and keep a cool head when customers occasionally get mad at you, your customers will keep coming back.

Extra Income from Discounts and Specials

Being a business owner means that you control just about every aspect of your business. Having this much control is a lot of responsibility, but it also means that an owner can strategize to make the most money possible. According to Hannah, she uses a few different methods to bring in as much money as possible. Hannah's shop offers regular discounts, for example, and has special discounts for repeat customers. "For owners of small dogs," Hannah says, "we offer a weekly bath for only $10. Other shops offer monthly baths for usually about $25, but monthly baths can be a lot of work because the dogs are so dirty after a month. Signing customers up for weekly baths means that we make $40 a dog rather than $25, and we also give customers more chances to tip us for doing a good job." Hannah's shop offers "spa treatments" and small extras as well, such as brushing a dog's teeth. These bonuses do not require much extra work but can bring in a lot of extra money.

Extra Income from the Sale of Retail Items

Hannah also uses her store space to sell retail items such as shampoos, dog vitamins, dog treats, and collars. (Retail is the sale of goods to individuals for their use, at stores or through other businesses.) She lets local retailers sell the items out of her shop, and she keeps part of the profit that she makes for each sale. Selling items this way means that she makes more money without having to do any extra work and without having to buy the items to stock her shelves. Though sales are not always good, there is no risk involved for her, so even only a few sales a month will still add money to her income.

"Being a business owner is about being strategic," Hannah says—and any strategic business owner can make a good living. MSNBC.com reports that self-employed dog groomers can earn up to $100,000 per year before expenses. These top earners definitely have good customer service skills and have been able to develop strategies to make the most money from their businesses.

AVERAGE SALARIES

Part of Hannah's success is due to her having chosen a good location for her business. Her shop is located in Westchester, New York, a highly populated suburb of New York City. "I originally thought of setting up a shop in New York City itself," Hannah says, "because there are a lot of dogs in New York." Hannah eventually, however, decided to establish her business in Westchester because the price of rent is significantly cheaper compared to New York City, and its location still offered her a large number of clients. (Rent is the amount of money a person pays to use a business space, apartment, home, or equipment.) Many of those clients also have high incomes, which means that they can afford to pay to have their pets groomed.

Not all dog groomers, however, will have the ability to establish a shop in an area like this. Likewise, most dog groomers do not have the kind of experience needed to open a shop and understand all that is necessary to make their shops as successful as Hannah's.

According to the U.S. Department of Labor, the average non-farm animal caretaker (which is what dog groomers are) makes nearly $23,000 a year—but when you consider that 35 percent of all non-farm animal caretakers work part time, the average salary of a full-time dog groomer is significantly higher than this. According to PayScale.com, for example, the average dog groomer makes more than $30,000 a year.

Some groomers seek to increase their earnings by selling dog care products.

RESEARCH PROJECT

Spend some time learning more about the various training options (apprenticeship, grooming schools, etc.) to become a dog groomer. Talk to groomers about how they trained for the field. Write a report that details what type of education is required, and the pros and cons of pursuing each type of education. Which training path is best for you?

TEXT-DEPENDENT QUESTIONS

1. What is an apprenticeship?
2. How does one become certified by the National Dog Groomers Association of America?
3. How much can a self-employed dog groomer earn a year?

WORDS TO UNDERSTAND

compassionate: being sympathetic and concerned about other people or animals that are suffering

detail-oriented: paying attention to the little things that make sure everything about a project or job is done well

stamina: the strength to continue for a long time

temperament: the sets of attitudes and behaviors that are typical to a person or animal

CHAPTER 5

KEY SKILLS AND METHODS OF EXPLORATION

WHAT ALL DOG GROOMERS NEED

"Dog grooming is a rewarding career," says Manuel Sandoval. "Grooming is a lot of hard work, and there is a lot to learn. There are so many breeds that it takes a long time before you have groomed them all and get used to all their different temperaments and personalities. For instance, pugs and greyhounds are easy to groom, and they have great personalities. They do not get excited easily, and they are generally pretty obedient. But shih tzus and certain kinds of terriers are nightmares. They bark a lot, and some of them are so small! A lot of time, they shake almost constantly while they get groomed."

Luckily, a lot of this type of knowledge can be learned on the job. But before you pick up a pair of scissors and begin to work on a dog, there are many other skills that you will need to learn.

According to Manuel, one of the best things about becoming a dog groomer is that you can try it out to see if it is a good fit for you. Since getting a job as a dog groomer doesn't take four years of college, you can give the profession a try and leave it if it is not the career for you. You could even work as a groomer part time while you're in college to test your interest and to make a little extra spending money.

"For a young person," Manuel says, "if you are deciding whether or not to go to college, I'd recommend you take a good look at yourself. I mean, what are your skills? What are you good at doing, really? And what do you like doing?"

Manuel makes an important point. Grooming dogs might sound like a lot of fun, but not everyone is cut out for it. Maybe you don't have the right skills for success in the field. Perhaps you don't like talking to people, which will make it hard to interact with customers (a big part of this job). Or you may like dogs—but the thought of pressing a dog's anal glands really grosses you out! On the other hand, maybe once you get used to the idea and get some experience, you'll discover it's really not such a big deal for you. Another point to keep in mind: Most skills can be learned with just a little effort. So don't give up if you're shy but really want to groom dogs. With a little practice, you might be able to turn yourself into a world-class communicator!

One of the best ways to figure out what you want to do in life is to try different things now. That way you can see for yourself what you really like best and what skills you already have. You might even surprise yourself!

Dog groomers need stamina in order to stand for long periods of time.

Like Rheya from Chapter 1, Manuel also began working with animals at a young age. "I volunteered at a vet's office when I was in high school," he says. "It was a great way to learn how to work with animals. I learned some simple grooming techniques there too. Vets do some of that also, so once I proved I could do it, the vet was happy to let me take care of any grooming they needed. But I think learning how to work with animals was the most important part. If you are calm, then they will be calm. If you are too loud or you get excited easy, working with animals may not be right for you. Animals can sense what you feel."

The U.S. Department of Labor identifies six traits that anyone working with animals should have:

- **Compassion.** All workers must be compassionate when dealing with animals and their owners. They should genuinely like animals and treat them with kindness. Dogs may be scared, and it is your job to calm them down and treat them gently and with love during this challenging time.

- **Customer service skills.** Animal care workers should understand pet owners' needs so they can provide services that leave the owners satisfied. Some animal care workers may need to deal with upset pet owners. They need good listening skills and patience to interact well with frustrated, demanding, or angry customers.

- **A detail-oriented personality.** Workers must be detail-oriented because they are often responsible for maintaining records and monitoring changes in animals' behavior. If you own a grooming business, you'll need to keep track of appointments, payments made by customers, and other important information.

- **Patience.** Animal caretakers need to be patient when dealing with animals that do not respond to commands.

- **Problem-solving skills.** Animal caretakers must have problem-solving skills when dealing with animal behaviors. They must assess whether the animals are responding to their methods and identify which methods are most successful.

- **Stamina.** Stamina is important for animal care workers because their work often involves kneeling, crawling, bending, and occasionally, lifting heavy animals and supplies.

According to Manuel, these are all skills that he uses daily, but patience is by far the most important skill to have. "If you are patient," he says, "then a scared or excited dog will likely calm down. Then you are less likely to make mistakes. Also, certain breeds have long coats, which need a lot of work and patience.

FIVE MYTHS ABOUT DOG GROOMING

Myth #1: Only certain dogs need to be groomed.

Fact: Some dogs (such as poodles and other long-haired breeds) need regular grooming, but all dogs need at least occasional grooming to keep them clean and attractive, reduce skin irritations, eliminate matted hair and excessive shedding, and reduce bad breath.

Myth #2: Dogs need to be bathed only once in a while.

Fact: Dogs should be bathed every two weeks or so—but sooner if they play in a muddy puddle or lose a run-in with a skunk. Baths also help dogs to shed less, smell better, and increase their resistance to some skin diseases. But don't wash your dog more than once a week! Doing so can remove protective natural oils on your dog's skin and dry out their skin.

Myth #3: It's ok to use human shampoo on your dog.

Fact: Human shampoo is bad for your dog! It can eliminate helpful oils, dry out the skin, and even damage a natural barrier on the skin that protects against infection. Ask your groomer or a veterinarian to recommend a quality dog shampoo.

Myth #4: Some dog breeds don't shed.

Fact: All dogs shed—most often during the spring and fall, but also when they are stressed, affected by environmental issues, or have a skin irritation. Regular grooming helps to reduce the amount of shedding.

Myth #5: Dogs need to be shaved during the summer to help them fight the heat.

Fact: This is untrue. A dog's thick coat helps to insulate it against the heat and regulate body temperature. Short-haired dogs need their coats to protect them from the hot sun.

If you are impatient while you work, the dog senses it. That isn't good for either you or the dog."

Examine yourself and be honest. If you already have some of these skills, then you are well on your way to an exciting life as a dog groomer. If you are not very strong in some of these areas, then now is the time to begin to practice these skills. They'll serve you well in other careers besides dog grooming!

It's a myth that only some dogs need to be groomed. The grooming process keeps dogs clean, healthy, and happy.

EXPLORING DOG GROOMING

There are many ways to explore a career in dog grooming. And unlike with many careers, you can get hands-on experience while you're still in your teens. Here are some suggestions to learn more about dog grooming.

TAKE SOME CLASSES

According to Manuel, some classes in high school, like biology, for example, can offer good knowledge that anyone working with animals should have. "I'm not a vet, and I don't pretend to be. But I use the stuff I learned in high school to help me understand a dog's body better. I do some reading too, whenever I can. It just helps me be the best I can. And I'm really interested."

Other classes will also be useful. Dog groomers need good communication skills, so taking speech classes will help you to build confidence and the skills to talk with people. Math classes will help you to tabulate customer bills and keep track of supplies and other items that you need. If you decide to open your own grooming company, business classes will teach you the basics of management and finances. Learning a foreign language can be fun, but it can also be useful if you have clients who do not speak the main language(s) of your country.

Local dog associations and pet care and supply stores may offer pet grooming classes for teens. If so, sign up and build your skills as a dog groomer.

GROOM A DOG

If you own a dog, this task is easy. If not, see if you can groom a friend's or neighbor's dog. But do some research before you start. YouTube.com offers dog

Learn how to groom a dog

Grooming your dog or a friend's pet is a good way to learn what groomers do each day.

grooming tutorials, and you should check out the Dog Grooming for Dummies Cheat Sheet at www.dummies.com/pets/dogs/dog-grooming-for-dummies-cheat-sheet for some tips. By doing basic tasks (brushing, bathing, shampooing, etc.), you'll get an understanding of what's involved in this career. If you become skilled at dog grooming, maybe you can even start a small neighborhood dog grooming business.

CONDUCT AN INFORMATION INTERVIEW WITH A DOG GROOMER

Participating in an information interview with a dog groomer is a great way to learn more about this career. During an information interview, you simply talk with a groomer and ask them questions about their educational background, work environment, job duties, and other topics that will help you decide if this is a good career for you. This type of interview can be conducted in person, on the phone, and via email or online video chat. Here are some questions to ask during the interview:

- Can you tell me about a day in your life on the job?
- What kinds of tools and equipment do you use on the job?
- Dogs can sometimes be aggressive or scared. How do you stay safe on the job?
- What are the most important personal and professional qualities for dog groomers? Business owners?
- What do you like best and least about your job?
- What is the future employment outlook for groomers? How is the field changing?
- What can I do now to prepare for the field?
- If you could go back in time, would you become a dog groomer again?

JOB SHADOW A DOG GROOMER

Job shadowing is kind of like an extended version of an information interview, except it is always done in person. During a job shadowing experience, you'll observe a dog groomer as they do their jobs. You'll watch them bathe and shampoo dogs, trim their nails, brush their teeth, and perform other dog grooming tasks. You'll get to watch them work with both challenging and easy-to-groom dogs. You can see how they interact with customers, and what it takes to run a business. You'll also get the chance to ask dog groomers questions about their work.

Setting Up an Information Interview or Job Shadowing Experience

There are several ways to set up these learning opportunities. If you own a dog, start with your groomer. Ask if they would be willing to participate in an information interview or job shadowing experience. If you don't own a dog, see if your dog-owning friends or neighbors can refer you to their groomer. You could also ask your school counselor for help. Finally, local and national pet grooming associations might be able to set up a learning opportunity with a dog groomer.

SOURCES OF ADDITIONAL EXPLORATION

Canadian Professional Pet Stylists
www.canpropetstylists.ca

International Professional Groomers, Inc.
www.ipgicmg.com

International Society of Canine Cosmetologists
www.iscceducation.com

National Dog Groomers Association of America
www.nationaldoggroomers.com

National Groomer Association of Canada
www.nationalgroomer.com

World Pet Association
www.worldpetassociation.org

Participating in an information interview or job shadowing experience might seem scary, but it's not. You'll find that most dog groomers love talking about their jobs.

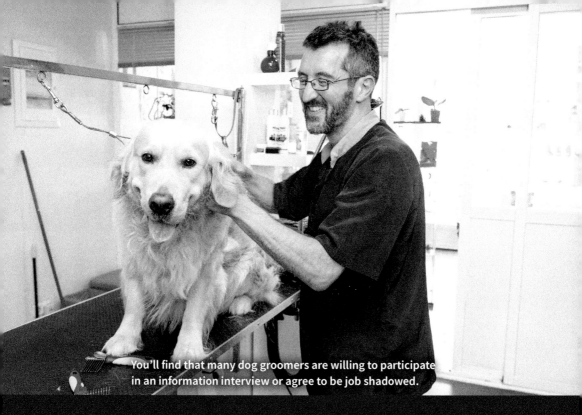

You'll find that many dog groomers are willing to participate in an information interview or agree to be job shadowed.

RESEARCH PROJECT

Learn as much as you can about dog grooming. Perhaps your local dog groomer can give you a few basic tips and let you watch them on the job. Under the supervision of a dog groomer or other knowledgeable adult, try your hand at grooming your dog or a neighbor's or friend's dog.

TEXT-DEPENDENT QUESTIONS

1. Why do dog groomers need good customer service skills?
2. Why is patience important for dog groomers?
3. What are three ways to explore the field of dog grooming?

WORDS TO UNDERSTAND

economy: activities related to production, consumption, and trade of services and goods in a city, state, region, or country

irresponsible: not caring about the consequences of one's actions

legislation: a proposed law

stifled: prevented or restrained someone from doing something

CHAPTER 6

LOOKING TO THE FUTURE

GROWING OPPORTUNITIES FOR DOG GROOMERS

If you are interested in becoming a dog groomer, then you need to know what the future of the dog grooming industry looks like. Luckily, due to the increasing number of homes with pets, dog groomers will continue to be in high demand for years to come.

Employment of animal care and service workers is projected to grow by 22 percent from 2016 to 2026, according to the U.S. Department of Labor (USDL). This is much faster than the average growth for all careers. The USDL reports that "many people consider their pets to be a part of their family and are willing to pay more for pet care than pet owners have in the past. As more households include companion pets, employment of animal care and service workers in the pet services industry will continue to grow. Employment of animal care and service workers in kennels, grooming shops, and pet stores is projected to increase in order to keep up with the growing demand for animal care."

FACTORS THAT MAY SLOW GROWTH

Although employment is currently good for dog groomers, several developments could reduce the number of job opportunities. The following sections provide more information.

NEW LAWS

While the future for dog groomers certainly looks bright, there are some laws being considered by states that could make becoming a dog groomer more difficult. In 2012, for example, California considered but did not pass a bill that would ask all existing and prospective dog groomers to become voluntarily certified and would subject grooming shops to random inspections (those that are unplanned) throughout the year. In 2018, lawmakers in New Jersey introduced legislation that, if passed, would require pet groomers to obtain a state groomer's license in order to work with animals. No states have passed bills like this, but they have been proposed in numerous states so far.

In general, dog groomers are split over the need for bills like this. On the one hand, dogs have been hurt and in some very rare instances killed by irresponsible groomers. Similarly, some groomers operating today are not qualified to be grooming dogs or handling animals, and yet they are allowed to operate due to the lack of regulation. On the other hand, the large growth of the industry could potentially be stifled. Some people argue that regulations

Dogs remain very popular family pets, which suggests that demand for groomers will continue to be strong.

like this wouldn't necessarily make grooming safer for the pets since most groomers who have injured animals would have been certified by the standards that the bill called for.

ECONOMIC TROUBLES

When the **economy** is strong, there are many jobs and people have disposable income (extra money) to spend on movies, flat-screen televisions, dining out, and, yes, pet care. If the economy goes into recession—a period of economic decline in one country, several countries, or worldwide, in which many banks fail, the real estate sector crashes, trade declines, and many people lose their jobs—people will have less money to spend on extras such as dog grooming.

To generate extra income, some dog groomers open doggie daycare facilities.

Learn more about the hidden costs associated with owning a pet.

They may groom their dog themselves or take their dog to a professional dog groomer only half as often as they did when they had more money. If a recession occurs, there will be fewer opportunities for dog groomers. Some may lose their jobs or have to charge less money to attract clients. Dog groomers can weather such challenges by expanding their business and the services they offer. For example, they might not just groom dogs but also cats and other animals. They might offer to walk dogs and care for dogs, cats, and other animals when their owners are on vacation. If they do these things, they'll increase their chances of keeping their business and making money. Finally, keep the following in mind: Recessions don't last forever. Eventually, the economy will improve and people will have more disposable income. When this occurs, there will be more opportunities for dog groomers.

A career as a groomer is an excellent option for people who love dogs, are attentive to detail, and have good hand-eye coordination.

INCREASING COMPETITION

For the right person, dog grooming can be an exciting and rewarding career. Currently, there is a strong need for groomers as the number of people who own dogs increases. But if too many people enter this field, demand for groomers will decrease and some people may lose their jobs. This happens in every career, so you just need to be ready for this possibility. Aspiring groomers should do some research before getting into the field. They should pick a town or neighborhood that seems to have a shortage of groomers so that they can get a lot of business. Offering additional services (cat grooming, dog walking, etc.) is another way to make yourself stand out from other dog groomers.

IN CLOSING

The people interviewed in this book are intelligent, driven, and passionate about what they are doing. (Someone who is passionate has a great love for what they are doing.) They all were willing to learn, even if learning didn't mean sitting in a college classroom. More importantly, for each of them, success didn't only mean the amount of money earned. For all of these dog groomers, success means pursuing what they are passionate about; it means learning all they can about themselves and their interests; it means defining their own standards of success.

For many people, college is the perfect choice and an important learning experience. Not only can it open the doors of certain careers, but it is also often the first experience that many young people have at living away from home without the safety and security of their parents. This is a great learning experience.

Unfortunately, many students go to college with no clear idea how to use the college experience to connect them with a lifetime of success. In some cases, young people go to college only because they feel pressured to do so by their peers or their parents. Many students leave college still with no idea of what they want from a career. And because of the staggering debt that many students have to acquire just to go to college, they may be in a far worse financial position than before.

What does success mean to you? Does it mean the amount of money you make? Or does it mean spending the majority of your time doing something you enjoy, something that makes you feel fulfilled and excited about your life? What do you most enjoy doing in life? What interests you?

There is no single right answer to these questions. The right answer for you will be based on honesty and a willingness to learn. Take advantage of every learning opportunity that comes your way, both in school and out of school. Learn as much as you can from your classes and schoolbooks, but also talk to your teachers. Pick their brains about their own experiences. Talk to your school counselor. Talk to other adults in your life. Read books on a variety of topics. Even fiction can give you a good idea what various jobs might be like. Check out jobs on the internet too. Volunteer in various ways. Be open to new ideas about both yourself and the world around you. Don't hesitate to try something new.

And because you're interested in dog grooming, participate in an information interview with a groomer, try grooming your dog, read books and watch videos about grooming, and try out other methods of exploration.

It's a big world out there, full of possibilities. Be willing to learn, work hard, and explore, no matter where life takes you!

Working as a dog groomer is an exciting and rewarding career, but it's not for everyone. Think carefully and do a lot of research as you consider potential career paths, and only pursue an occupation that makes you excited about going to work every day.

RESEARCH PROJECT

Talk to dog groomers about their businesses. Ask them to describe some of the challenges they face in running their business. Ask them how they think the field will change in the future, and what young people can do now to prepare for these changes. Write a report that summarizes their responses. Keep these things in mind as you train to become a dog groomer and, potentially, a business owner.

TEXT-DEPENDENT QUESTIONS

1. Why is the employment outlook good for dog groomers?
2. What factors could cause job growth to slow?
3. What does it mean to be passionate?

accreditation: The process of being evaluated and approved by a governing body as providing excellent coursework, products, or services. Quality college and university educational programs are accredited.

application materials: Items, such as a cover letter, resume, and letters of recommendation, that one provides to employers when applying for a job or an internship.

apprenticeship: A formal training program that combines classroom instruction and supervised practical experience. Apprentices are paid a salary that increases as they obtain experience.

associate's degree: A degree that requires a two-year course of study after high school.

bachelor's degree: A degree that requires a four-year course of study after high school.

certificate: A credential that shows a person has completed specialized education, passed a test, and met other requirements to qualify for work in a career or industry. College certificate programs typically last six months to a year.

certification: A credential that one earns by passing a test and meeting other requirements. Certified workers have a better chance of landing a job than those who are not certified. They also often earn higher salaries than those who are not certified.

community college: A private or public two-year college that awards certificates and associates degrees.

consultant: An experienced professional who is self-employed and provides expertise about a particular subject.

cover letter: A one-page letter in which a job seeker summarizes their educational and professional background, skills, and achievements, as well as states their interest in a job.

doctoral degree: A degree that is awarded to an individual who completes two or three additional years of education after earning a master's degree. It is also known as a **doctorate**.

for-profit business: One that seeks to earn money for its owners.

fringe benefits: A payment or non-financial benefit that is given to a worker in addition to salary. These consist of cash bonuses for good work, paid vacations and sick days, and health and life insurance.

information interview: The process of interviewing a person about their career, whether in person, by phone, online, or by email.

internship: A paid or unpaid learning opportunity in which a student works at a business to obtain experience for anywhere from a few weeks to a year.

job interview: A phone, internet, or in-person meeting in which a job applicant presents their credentials to a hiring manager.

job shadowing: The process of following a worker around while they do their job, with the goal of learning more about a particular career and building one's network.

licensing: Official permission that is granted by a government agency to a person in a particular field (nursing, engineering, etc.) to practice in their profession. Licensing requirements typically involve meeting educational and experience requirements, and sometimes passing a test.

master's degree: A two-year, graduate-level degree that is earned after a student first completes a four-year bachelor's degree.

mentor: An experienced professional who provides advice to a student or inexperienced worker (mentee) regarding personal and career development.

minimum wage: The minimum amount that a worker can be paid by law.

nonprofit organization: A group that uses any profits it generates to advance its stated goals (protecting the environment, helping the homeless, etc.). It is not a corporation or other for-profit business.

professional association: An organization that is founded by a group of people who have the same career (engineers, professional hackers, scientists, etc.) or who work in the same industry (information technology, health care, etc.).

professional network: Friends, family, coworkers, former teachers, and others who can help you find a job.

recruiting firm: A company that matches job seekers with job openings.

registered apprenticeship: A program that meets standards of fairness, safety, and training established by the U.S. government or local governments.

resume: A formal summary of one's educational and work experience that is submitted to a potential employer.

salary: Money one receives for doing work.

scholarship: Money that is awarded to students to pay for college and other types of education; it does not have to be paid back.

self-employed: Working for oneself as a small business owner, rather than for a corporation or other employer. Self-employed people must generate their own income and provide their own fringe benefits (such as health insurance).

soft skills: Personal abilities that people need to develop to be successful on the job—communication, work ethic, teamwork, decision-making, positivity, time management, flexibility, problem-solving, critical thinking, conflict resolution, and other skills and traits.

technical college: A public or private college that offers two- or four-year programs in practical subjects, such as the trades, information technology, applied sciences, agriculture, and engineering.

union: An organization that seeks to gain better wages, benefits, and working conditions for its members. Also called a **labor union** or **trade union**.

work-life balance: A healthy balance of time spent on the job and time spent with family and on leisure activities.

FURTHER READING

Gould, Sue. *The Dog Groomer's Manual: A Definitive Guide to the Science, Practice and Art of Dog Grooming*. Wiltshire, U.K.: Crowood Press, 2014.

Hajeski, Nancy. *Every Dog: A Book of Over 450 Breeds*. Richmond Hill, O.N. Canada: Firefly Books, 2016.

Mattinson, Pippa. *Choosing the Perfect Puppy*. London, U.K.: Ebury Press, 2017.

Shojai, Amy. *Dog Facts: The Pet Parent's A-to-Z Home Care Encyclopedia: Puppy to Adult, Diseases & Prevention, Dog Training, Veterinary Dog Care, First Aid, Holistic Medicine*. McKinney, Tex.: Furry Muse Publications, 2016.

INTERNET RESOURCES

www.bls.gov/ooh/personal-care-and-service/animal-care-and-service-workers.htm This section of the *Occupational Outlook Handbook* features information on job duties, educational requirements, salaries, and the employment outlook for animal care workers.

https://work.chron.com/dog-grooming-jobs-teens-26497.html This website provides advice for teens on how to groom a dog.

https://people.com/pets/what-to-know-before-you-set-up-a-grooming-session-for-your-pet A dog groomer answers questions about the dog grooming process.

www.akc.org/dog-breeds This website from the American Kennel Club provides information on a variety of dog breeds and includes photos.

EDUCATIONAL VIDEO LINKS

Chapter 1
Learn more about what it's like to own a dog grooming business: http://x-qr.net/1JD3

Chapter 2
Dog groomers discuss their work: http://x-qr.net/1JF7

Chapter 4
Discover what goes on in dog grooming courses at The College of Animal Welfare in the United Kingdom: http://x-qr.net/1Kfq

Chapter 5
Learn how to groom a dog: http://x-qr.net/1KFU

Chapter 6
Learn more about the hidden costs associated with owning a pet: http://x-qr.net/1LuJ

INDEX

AUTHOR BIOGRAPHIES

Andrew Morkes has been a writer and editor for more than twenty-five years. He is the author of more than twenty-five books about college planning and careers, including all of the titles in this series, many titles in the Careers in the Building Trades series, the *Vault Career Guide to Social Media*, and *They Teach That in College!?: A Resource Guide to More Than 100 Interesting College Majors*, which was selected as one of the best books of the year by the library journal *Voice of Youth Advocates*. He is also the author and publisher of "The Morkes Report: College and Career Planning Trends" blog.

Christie Marlowe lives in Binghamton, New York, where she works as a writer and web designer. She has a degree in literature, cares strongly about the environment, and spends three or more nights a week wailing on her Telecaster.

PHOTO CREDITS